Map 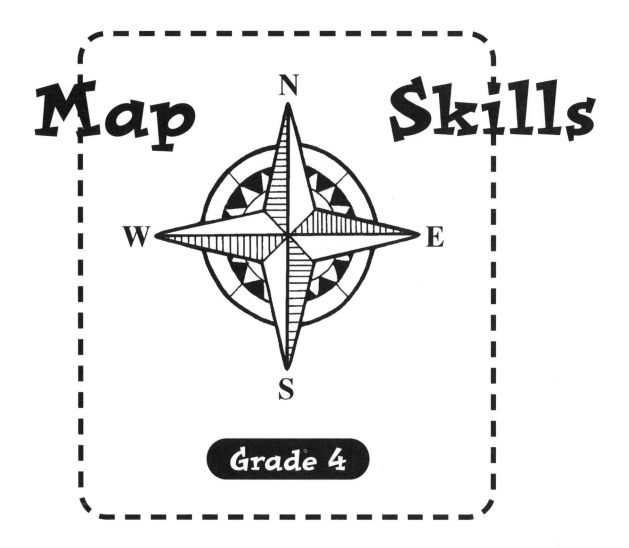 Skills

Grade 4

by Sharon Thompson

Carson-Dellosa Publishing Company, Inc.
Greensboro, North Carolina

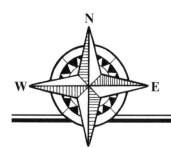

Credits

Project Director

Tara Poitras

Editors

Whitney Brooks
Erin Proctor

Inside Illustrators

Milton Hall
Bill Neville
Erik Huffine

Cover Design

Matthew Van Zomeren

Cover Photos

Mountain High Maps®
Copyright © 1993 Digital
Wisdom, Inc.
Photo www.comstock.com

*Special thanks to the teachers of Hamilton Elementary–
Carol McMillen, Carol Griffiths, Marlys Heisler, and Lisa Gray–
for their assistance with this project.*

Table of Contents

Introduction

Students may not realize it, but they use map skills every day. Walking to a friend's house and shopping at the mall both require map-skill knowledge. The activities in this book will teach students how to read maps and how to apply this knowledge to their everyday lives. Students will be introduced to a variety of map types. They will learn how to use a compass rose and map key, how to trace a route, how to measure distance on a map, and how to make maps of their own. A full-page US map with the states and capitals labeled is included in the back of the book to help with some of the activities.

Additionally, this book covers different parts of the world, as well as interesting geographical facts about the world. Students will learn just how important map skills are to them as they learn more about the world around them. The activities require thinking, drawing, and writing (and in some cases, an atlas and ruler). The activities in this book will help students develop an understanding of, and an appreciation for, map skills in their lives.

Make Map-Skill Lessons Come Alive!

Below is a list of activities and suggestions that can be used in addition to those included in this book. These ideas can be used as written or can be tailored to fit your classroom's needs.

1. Create hands-on maps
Be creative! Items in the classroom, kitchen, and probably the trunk of your car can make mapmaking and map-skill learning more fun and meaningful! For example, make an edible physical map from packaged sugar dough, with chocolate drop candies for mountains, blue frosting for bodies of water, etc.

2. Get students moving
Use students as "human maps" or globes. To demonstrate a map scale, have two students act as locations—such as two states— by standing at opposite ends of the classroom. Provide students with a scale so the class can determine the real distance between the two locations. Or, take students to the mall, a local park, or the playground to practice directions, map coordinates, and mapmaking.

3. Design a geo-center
Create a designated classroom center with students' projects and geography manipulatives, such as an inflatable globe, flash cards, maps, and an atlas.

4. Provide a laminated map for each student
Whether using a commercially made or a copied/laminated map, invest in maps that students can hold, write on, and refer to throughout lessons.

5. Keep a binder or pizza-box portfolio for each student
Clean pizza boxes are a great way to house map projects, reports, notes, and worksheets. Place them in the geo-center for safekeeping and convenient reference.

Super Spellers

There are nine students in the spelling bee. Read the directions below and use the compass rose to find out where each student is sitting. Use the **cardinal directions,** north, south, east, and west, and the **intermediate directions,** northeast, northwest, southeast, and southwest. Write the students' names in the boxes provided.

1.	Devin is in the southeast corner.
2.	Judy is west of Devin.
3.	Alyssa is #8.
4.	Beatrice is just north of Devin.
5.	Jeff is north of Beatrice.
6.	Drew is just south of Alyssa.
7.	Frank is in the northwest corner.
8.	Karen is just south of Frank.
9.	Sam is in the southwest corner.

Name _____

Wild Goose Chase

Peter's pet goose escaped from its cage. Starting at the arrow, trace a line to follow the wild goose chase.

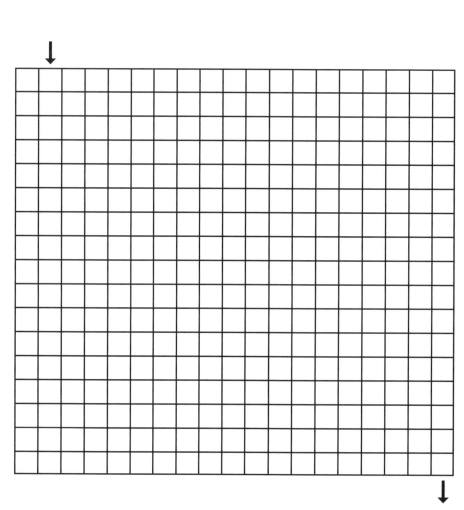

1. Go 4 south.
2. Go 5 east.
3. Go 6 south.
4. Go 3 east.
5. Go 3 south.

6. Go 2 west.
7. Go 2 south.
8. Go 5 east.
9. Go 2 south.

10. Go 2 east.
11. Go 2 north.
12. Go 4 east.
13. Go 2 south.

Sophie's New House

Floor plans show the layout of a house or building. Below is a floor plan of Sophie's new house. Study the floor plan and answer the questions below.

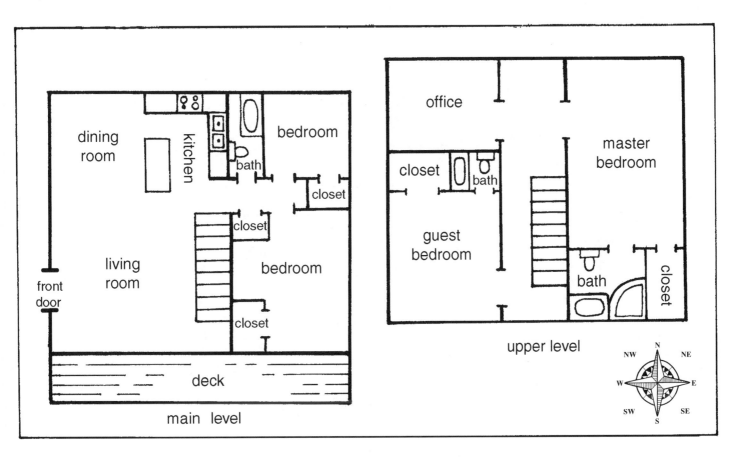

1. How many levels does Sophie's new house have? _____
2. The deck is on the _____ level.
3. How many bathrooms are there?_____
4. The bathroom on the main level is _____ of the kitchen.
5. How many closets does Sophie's house have? _____
6. The master bedroom is _____ of the office.
7. Does the office lead into the bathroom? _____
8. On what level is the guest bedroom?_____

Name_____

Captain's Log

Captain Kris is a spaceship captain. He must use a **grid** and **coordinates** (the letters and numbers along the grid) to determine his location in space on a given day. Read the Captain's Log below and fill in the blanks.

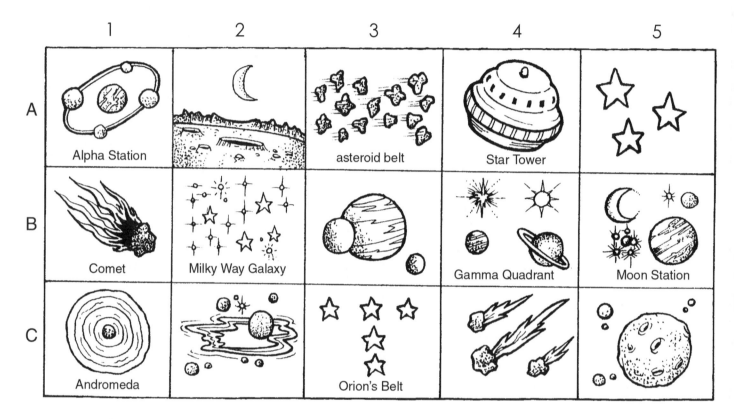

Captain's Log

		Coordinates
Day 1	We left the Alpha Station.	_____
Day 2	We stopped at _____ _____.	C-3
Day 3	We arrived at Andromeda.	_____
Day 4	Stopped for refueling at Gamma Quadrant	_____
Day 5	Visited the Moon Station	_____
Day 6	Went to the _____ _____ _____.	B-2
Day 7	Flew through an asteroid belt	_____
Day 8	Arrived at the _____ _____ for ship repairs	A-4

Camp Getaway

Below is a map of the local summer camp. Using the grid and coordinates on the map, follow the steps to find out the route of the scavenger hunt. Fill in the blanks below.

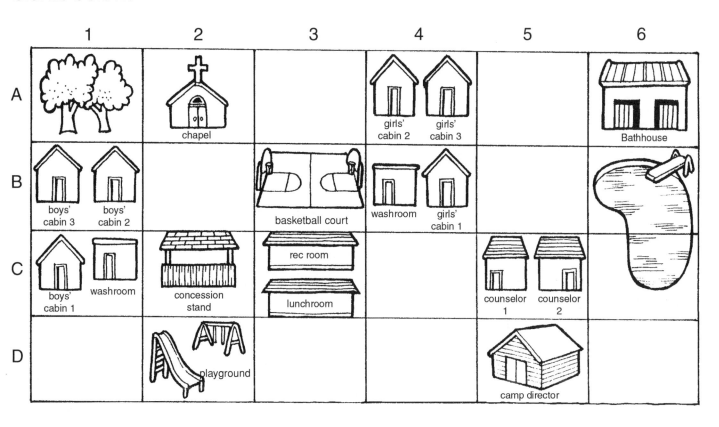

1. The scavenger hunt will begin at the rec room. From there, go to D-5.

   _____ _____

2. From D-5, go to D-2. _____

3. From D-2, go to B-6. _____

4. Next, go to girls' cabin 2 and girls' cabin 3 at coordinate _____.

5. The next stop is back at C-3 but not at the rec room. _____

6. Go to the chapel next at coordinate _____.

7. From there, stop at boys' cabin 3 at coordinate _____.

8. Next go to B-3. _____ _____

9. Your last stop is at C-2. _____ _____

How Far?

A **map scale** is used to show distance on a map. A map cannot be shown at actual size, so it must be made smaller to fit on paper. Juan's family is planning a vacation. His dad does not want to drive more than 600 miles. Using the scale and the map, measure from the points to find out how far each site is from Juan's home. Answer the questions.

1 inch = 600 miles

1. Is the Grand Canyon within 600 miles of Juan's home? _____

2. Which is closer to Juan's home, the St. Louis Arch or the Baseball Hall of Fame?

   _____

3. Which is farther from Juan's home, the Space Needle or the Grand Canyon?

   _____

4. How far is Mt. Rushmore from Juan's home?

   _____

Map Key

St. Louis Arch

Mt. Rushmore

Baseball Hall of Fame

Grand Canyon

Juan's home

Space Needle

Traveling through the Black Hills

People use **road maps** to drive from one place to another. The map below shows highways, routes, and interstates near Mt. Rushmore in South Dakota. Study the map and answer the questions about traveling through the Black Hills.

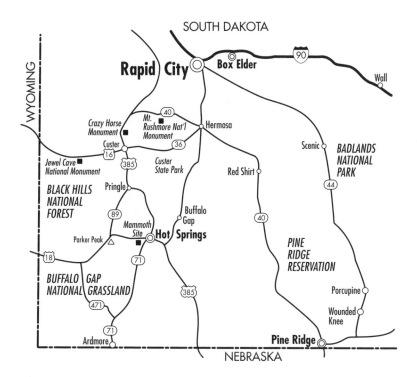

1. Which route runs from Hot Springs to Ardmore? _____

2. What two highways lead from South Dakota to Wyoming? _____ and _____

3. Which route runs through Buffalo Gap National Grassland? _____

4. Which route runs from Red Shirt to Pine Ridge? _____

5. Which interstate runs from Wall to Box Elder? _____

6. Which route runs from Red Shirt to Mt. Rushmore? _____

7. Which highway goes from Custer to Jewel Cave National Monument? _____

8. What route goes from Rapid City to Scenic? _____

Name_____

Farmington Field Trip

The students at Farmington School are pen pals with students at Bradley University. The Bradley students decided to visit Farmington School. Use the map to fill in the blanks.

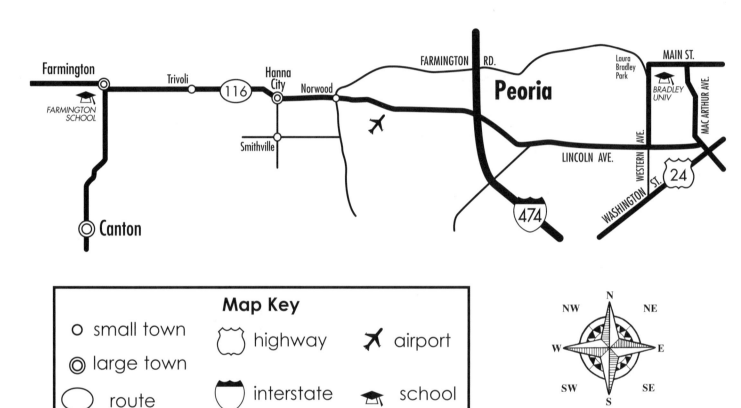

1. From Bradley University, take Farmington Road, heading northwest past _____ _____ Park.

2. Stay on _____ Road until you reach Norwood.

3. At Norwood, take route _____ west through Hanna City and _____ to Farmington.

4. Farmington is _____ (direction) of Peoria.

5. Hanna City is north of _____.

6. An airport is located _____ of Farmington.

7. What is the next large town south of Farmington? _____

8. What interstate is shown on this map?_____

Platte Parade

A **route** is a path to and from a location. A local scout group is marching in a parade in Davis Township. Read the directions below and trace the route on the map.

1. The parade starts at the south edge of Newton going southeast on Road 1150.
2. It turns east onto 2770, then turns south again on 1200.
3. It continues on this road until 2700. It turns west onto 2700.
4. Next, the parade turns south on 1150. At the end of this road, the parade turns west onto 2600. It stays on this road to Irish Spring Road.
5. The parade turns north onto Irish Spring Road and heads northeast back to Newton.

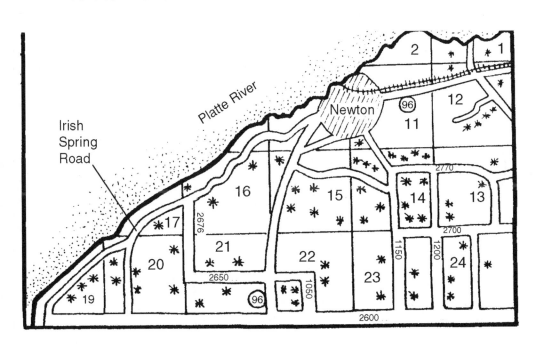

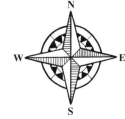

Map Key

○ highway

* house

‡ railroad

Answer the following questions about Davis Township.
1. What river borders Davis Township? _____ _____
2. What highway is in Davis Township? _____ .
3. The railroad runs through which sections? _____ and _____
4. What road runs through the middle of section 23? _____
5. Which section has the most houses? _____
6. How many houses are in that section? _____

Map the Solar System

The map below shows the orbits of planets in the solar system. Use an encyclopedia or reference book to research the solar system. Using the map key, draw each planet on its correct orbit around the sun. Then, trace each orbit in a different color.

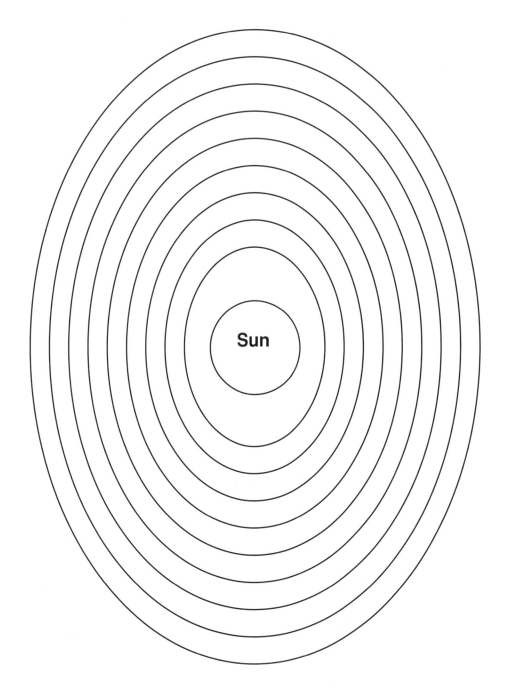

Map Key

E   Earth

J   Jupiter

Ma   Mars

Me   Mercury

N   Neptune

P   Pluto

S   Saturn

U   Uranus

V   Venus

Sun

Mapping Products

A **product map** uses symbols to show which crops grow in a certain place. Below are product maps of Wisconsin and Texas. Compare the two maps and answer the questions that follow.

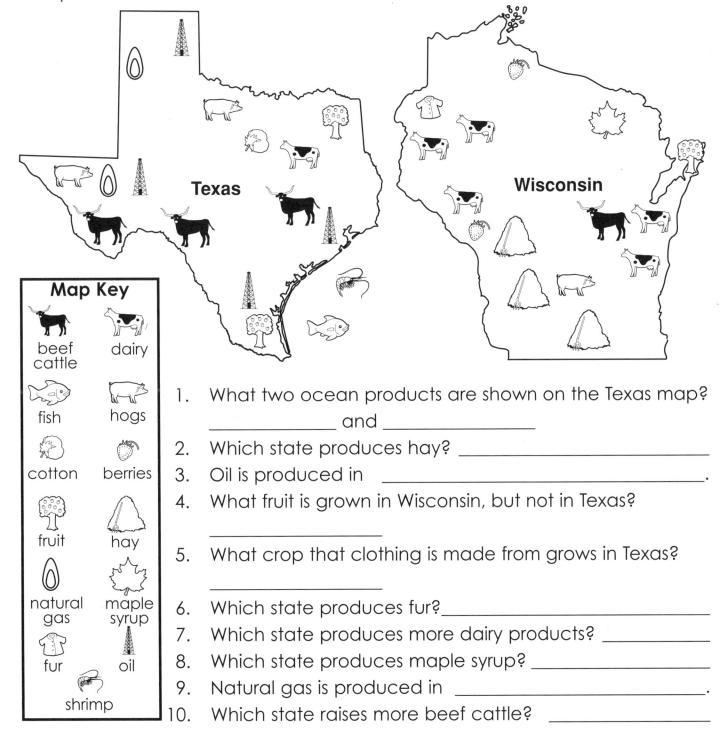

Map Key

beef cattle   dairy

fish   hogs

cotton   berries

fruit   hay

natural gas   maple syrup

fur   oil

shrimp

1. What two ocean products are shown on the Texas map? _____ and _____

2. Which state produces hay? _____

3. Oil is produced in _____.

4. What fruit is grown in Wisconsin, but not in Texas? _____

5. What crop that clothing is made from grows in Texas? _____

6. Which state produces fur?_____

7. Which state produces more dairy products? _____

8. Which state produces maple syrup? _____

9. Natural gas is produced in _____.

10. Which state raises more beef cattle? _____

It's Raining! It's Pouring!

Compare the **precipitation maps**, or rainfall maps, below of Arizona and the main island of Hawaii. These maps use patterns to show areas with varying amounts of rainfall.

Annual Rainfall

Hawaii

Arizona

Map Key

☐ less than 25 inches

☐ 25 to 200 inches

☐ more than 200 inches

Kamuela · Honokaa
Kailua Kona · Hilo

Map Key

☐ less than 8 inches

☐ 8 to 16 inches

☐ more than 16 inches

Flagstaff
Phoenix ★
Yuma
Tucson

1. According to the map keys, which state receives more rainfall? _____

2. Honokaa, Hawaii, receives how much annual rainfall? _____

3. What does ☐ on the Arizona map represent? _____

_____

4. What does ☐ on Hawaii's map represent? _____

_____

5. What city is in the driest part of Hawaii? _____

6. What city on the Arizona map receives the most annual rainfall? _____

7. How much annual rainfall does Tucson, Arizona, receive? _____

8. How much annual rainfall does Kailua Kona, Hawaii, receive? _____

Name_____

Airport Delays

Weather maps are used to show what the weather may be like at a certain time. Weather conditions such as fog, thunderstorms, rain, and snow can cause travel delays at airports. Use the weather map of the continental United States to answer the questions.

1. Will there be a delay at the airport in Miami? _____

2. What kind of weather does Minneapolis have? _____

3. Which airport is more likely to have a delay, St. Louis or Atlanta? _____

4. What cities have partly cloudy conditions? _____, _____, and _____ _____.

5. What is the weather like in New York? _____

6. Which two cities have fog?_____ _____ and _____

7. Could there be a delay in Denver? _____

8. If you were flying from Los Angeles to Denver to Chicago, do you think your flight would be on time? _____ Why or why not? _____
_____

"Weather" It's Hot or Not

There are many different conditions in the atmosphere that cause weather.
Study the weather map and the map key to answer the questions below.

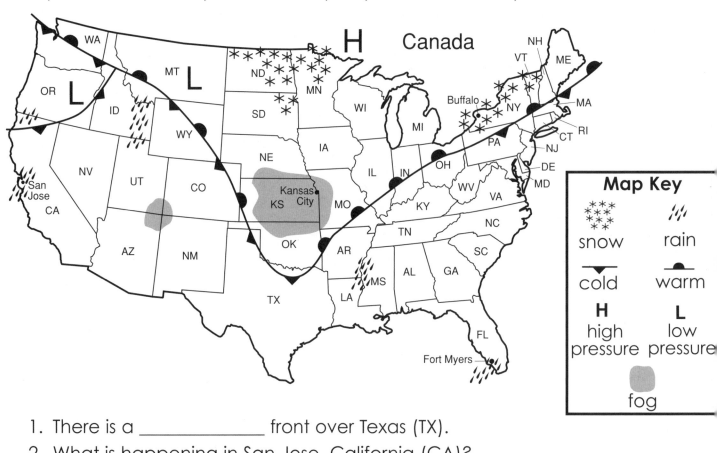

1. There is a _____ front over Texas (TX).
2. What is happening in San Jose, California (CA)? _____
3. In what city in New York (NY) is it snowing? _____
4. What might cause airplanes in Kansas City, Kansas (KS), to have trouble
   taking off or landing? _____
5. What type of front is stretching across Missouri (MO)? _____
6. What three midwestern states are experiencing snow? _____,
   _____ _____, and _____ _____
7. What city in Florida (FL) is receiving rain? _____ _____
8. Where is the high pressure area? _____
9. What states are low pressure areas? _____ and _____

What's in a Word?

Below are some pictures and descriptions of terms or words used in geography. Study the pictures and read the definitions. Then, find the landforms in the picture on the next page and match each landform with its name.

A **mountain** is a high, rugged landform.

A **river** is a moving body of water.

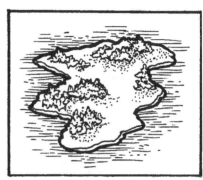

An **island** is land with water on all sides.

A **valley** is the low land between mountains.

A **plateau** is a high landform that is flat on top.

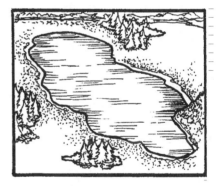

A **lake** is an inland body of water.

An **ocean** is the largest body of water on Earth.

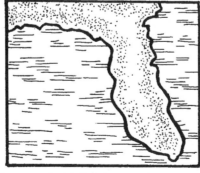

A **peninsula** is a piece of land that juts out into the water.

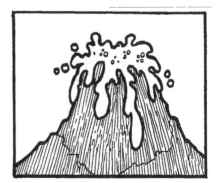

A **volcano** is a mountain that spews lava from inside the earth.

Geographic Features

Find on the map the geographic land features that are listed below. Then, write the numbers from the list on the correct features.

Features
1. lake
2. river
3. mountain
4. valley
5. volcano
6. plateau
7. peninsula
8. island
9. ocean

Name_____

Matching Maps

Read each group of terms. Circle the one that does not belong with the others. Then, write what the other three have in common on the line. You may use an atlas. The first one is done for you.

1. oceans_____
   A. Pacific Ocean   C. Arctic Ocean
   B. Atlantic Ocean   (D.) Asia

2. _____
   A. California   C. Mississippi River
   B. Amazon River   D. Nile River

3. _____
   A. Australia   C. Canada
   B. Africa   D. South America

4. _____
   A. Oklahoma   C. Virginia
   B. Illinois   D. Canada

5. _____
   A. Pikes Peak   C. Mount Everest
   B. Hawaii   D. Mount Fuji

6. _____
   A. Red Sea   C. Lake Michigan
   B. Salt Lake   D. Lake Okeechobee

7. _____
   A. Atlanta   C. Seattle
   B. Maryland   D. Los Angeles

8. _____
   A. Black Sea   C. Dead Sea
   B. Mediterranean Sea   D. Sahara Desert

Name_____

Physical Features

A **physical map** shows geographic features such as mountains, lakes, and rivers. Look at the physical map of the United States to answer the questions below.

1. The Great Lakes are located in the northern United States. Name them.

   _____ _____, _____ _____, _____ _____,
   _____ _____ and _____ _____.

2. What land region is in the center of the United States? _____ _____

3. What mountain range is located just west of the Interior Plains?

   _____ _____

4. What mountain range is located in California? _____ _____

5. What oceans border the United States? _____ _____
   and _____ _____

6. What body of water lies south of the United States? _____ ___ _____

7. The two countries that border the United States are _____
   and _____.

8. What desert is shown? _____ _____

9. Which US state is a group of islands? _____

Name_____

Mapping Africa

Use an atlas to make a physical map of Africa below. Label the following features on the map and then follow the directions below.

Ahaggar Mountains
Atlas Mountains
Congo River
Lake Chad

Lake Tanganyika
Lake Victoria
Namib Desert
Nile River
Madagascar (island)

Mediterranean Sea
Red Sea
Sahara Desert
Strait of Gibraltar

1. Color the deserts orange.

2. Draw brown triangles for the mountains.

3. Draw blue lines and circles for the rivers and lakes.

4. Draw a green line on the equator.

5. Draw red lines on the tropic of Cancer and the tropic of Capricorn.

Name_____

Mapping Montana

Below is a blank map of the state of Montana. Practice your mapping skills by adding the items listed below to the map. Use an atlas to help you.

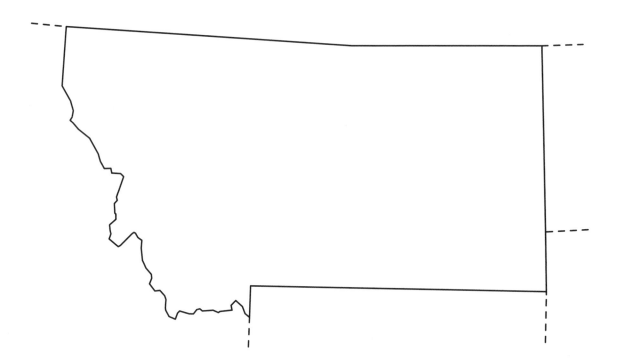

1. Draw brown triangles for the Rocky Mountains, and trace the Bitterroot Range in green.
2. Place a large red dot on the following cities: Butte, Bozeman, Great Falls, Missoula, and Billings.
3. What is Montana's capital? _____ Place a green dot on it.
4. Draw in the Missouri River and the Yellowstone River with blue pencils.
5. Add Fort Peck Lake and Flathead Lake to the map with purple pencils.
6. Label the states that border Montana.
7. Label the country that borders Montana.
8. Label Yellowstone National Park and Glacier National Park in blue.

Mapping Your State

Political maps show governmental divisions of land such as countries or states. Use an atlas for reference and create a political map of your state. Include the state's boundaries. Use colored dots to mark large cities and a star to mark the capital.

Political Map

Now, create a physical map of your state. Add land features such as rivers, lakes, deserts, or mountains. Use an atlas for reference.

Physical Map

Name _____

South America Scramble

The names of scrambled countries and **dependencies** of South America are listed below. Look at the map of South America, then unscramble each name and write it on the line provided.

1. ELCIH _____
2. URPE _____
3. GAPYRAUA _____
4. RBIZLA _____
5. OLMBAIOC _____
6. YGNAUA _____
7. DERCUAO _____

8. GAUURYU _____
9. NEIAGRTAN _____
10. EMSURINA _____
11. CEHFRN AGIANU _____
12. ZNEUEEAVL _____
13. VLOBIIA _____

Write the countries in alphabetical order on the lines below.

_____
_____
_____
_____
_____
_____
_____
_____
_____
_____
_____
_____

Where on Earth? Part 1

Lines of latitude are imaginary lines that run east to west around the earth. These lines are measured in degrees. The **equator** is 0° latitude, and it divides the earth into two halves, the **northern hemisphere** and the **southern hemisphere**. The map below shows lines of latitude in 20° segments. Use this map to answer the following questions.

1. At what degree north can you find the north pole? _____
2. What is the 0° latitude line called? _____
3. At what degree south can you find the south pole? _____
4. The portion of the globe from 0° latitude to the north pole is the
    _____ hemisphere.
5. The portion of the globe from 0° latitude to the south pole is the
    _____ hemisphere.

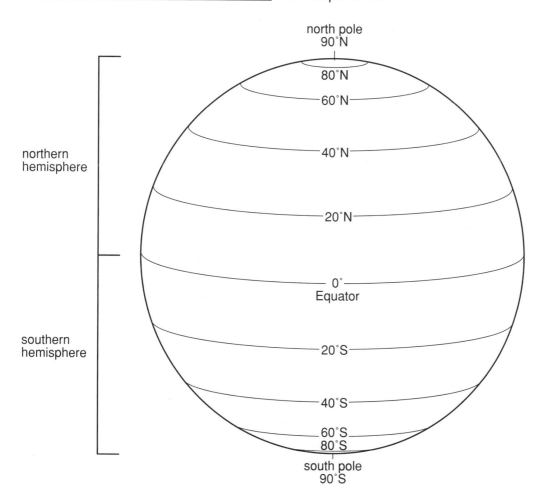

Where on Earth? Part 2

Lines of longitude are imaginary lines that run north to south on the Earth. They are measured in degrees and are used with lines of latitude to help locate places on the globe. The **prime meridian** is 0° longitude. Along with **180° longitude**, it divides the Earth into eastern and western hemispheres. The world **time zones** begin at this line. The map below shows lines of longitude in 20° segments. Use the map to answer the following questions.

1. What is the line at 0° longitude called? _____ _____

2. The portion of the globe from the prime meridian east to 180° longitude is the _____ hemisphere.

3. The portion of the globe from the prime meridian west to 180° longitude is the _____ hemisphere.

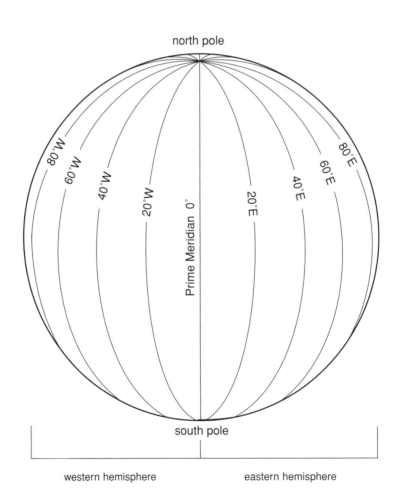

Two Hemispheres

Study the map to the right. Write the name
of each continent beside its letter below.
You may use an atlas.

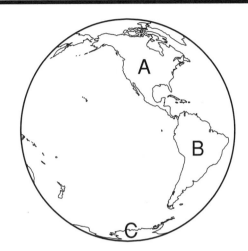

A. _ _ _ _ _   _ _ _ _ _ _ _
    1   2   3   4

B. _ _ _ _ _   _ _ _ _ _ _ _
    5   6   7

C. _ _ _ _ _ _ _ _ _ _
      8

Use the letter code above to solve the puzzle below. The continents above (or
parts of them) are found in the:

W _ _ _ _ _ _   _ _ _ _ _ P _ _ _ _
   7 5 8 7 2 1   6 7 3 4 5   6 7 2 7

Study the map to the right. Write the name
of each continent beside its letter below.
You may use an atlas.

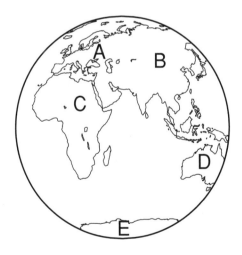

A. _ _ _ _ _ _
    1   2

B. _ _ _ _
     3

C. _ _ _ _ _ _
    4   5

D. _ _ _ _ _ _ _ _ _
       6

E. _ _ _ _ _ _ _ _ _ _
       7

Use the letter code above to solve the puzzle below. The continents above (or
parts of them) are found in the:

_ _ _ _ _ _ N   H _ M _ _ _ H _ _ _
 1 4 3 6 1 5   1   7 3 2 1 5 1

East and West

The **prime meridian** (0˚ longitude) and **180˚ longitude** are a set of imaginary lines that run north to south. These lines divide the earth into two halves called the **eastern hemisphere** and the **western hemisphere**. Study the maps below and circle the correct answers to complete the sentences at the bottom of the page. Use an atlas or world map to identify the continents shown.

western hemisphere

eastern hemisphere

1.	North America is in the	eastern	western	hemisphere.
2.	Asia is mostly in the	eastern	western	hemisphere.
3.	Africa is in the	eastern	western	hemisphere.
4.	South America is in the	eastern	western	hemisphere.
5.	Europe is in the	eastern	western	hemisphere.
6.	Australia is mostly in the	eastern	western	hemisphere.

Locating Landmarks

Find each landmark by locating its number on the map below. Then, fill in the missing information. Estimate the latitude and longitude of the cities where the landmarks or events are located or write the cities' names that match the coordinates given.

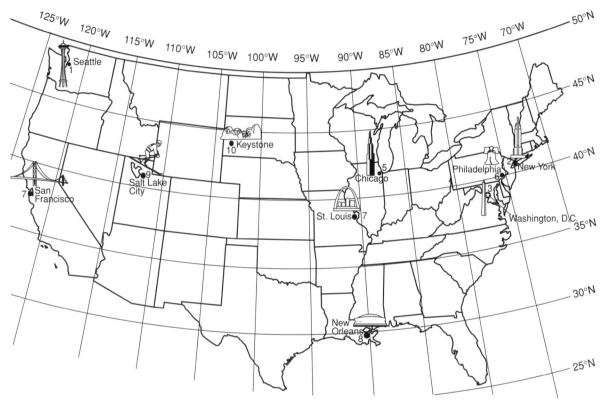

	Landmark	Latitude	Longitude	City
1.	Space Needle	48°N	122°W	_____
2.	Empire State Building	____	____	New York
3.	Washington Monument	39°N	77°W	_____
4.	Gateway Arch	____	____	St. Louis
5.	Sears Tower	____	____	Chicago
6.	Liberty Bell	40°N	76°W	_____
7.	Golden Gate Bridge	38°N	122°W	_____
8.	Superdome	____	____	New Orleans
9.	2002 Winter Olympics	____	____	Salt Lake City
10.	Mt. Rushmore	44°N	104°W	_____

Locating Continents

Below is a world map with all seven continents. Each continent is marked with a dot. Find the latitude and longitude of each dot and write these numbers on the lines beside the appropriate continent. You may use an atlas.

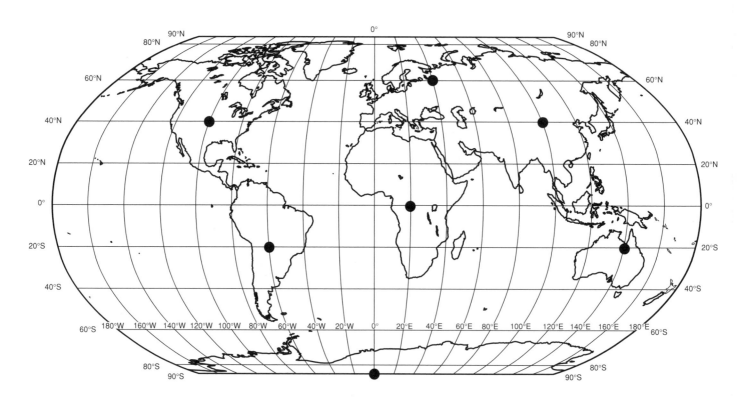

		Latitude	Longitude
1.	North America	_____	_____
2.	South America	_____	_____
3.	Africa	_____	_____
4.	Europe	_____	_____
5.	Asia	_____	_____
6.	Australia	_____	_____
7.	Antarctica	_____	_____

latitude and longitude

Presidential Birth States

Use the latitude and longitude map of the United States to locate the birthplaces of US presidents. Use the latitude and longitude given to find the state of each president listed. Write the name of the state on the line provided. You may use an atlas to identify state names.

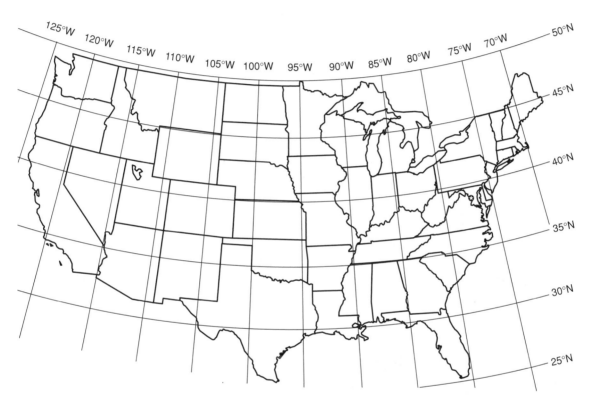

President	Latitude	Longitude	Birth State
1. Ronald Reagan	37°N–43°N	87°W–92°W	_____
2. Harry S. Truman	36°N–41°N	90°W–95°W	_____
3. Lyndon Johnson	26°N–36°N	94°W–107°W	_____
4. Abraham Lincoln	36°N–38°N	82°W°–89°W	_____
5. Herbert Hoover	41°N–44°N	90°W–97°W	_____
6. John F. Kennedy	42°N–43°N	70°W–73°W	_____
7. James Buchanan	40°N–42°N	75°W–81°W	_____
8. Jimmy Carter	31°N–35°N	81°W–86°W	_____
9. Richard Nixon	33°N–42°N	115°W–124°W	_____
10. George Washington	36°N–39°N	76°W–83°W	_____

Shape Up!

Identify the shaded US states. Then, write each state's name on the line below its map. Use an atlas or the US map on page 45.

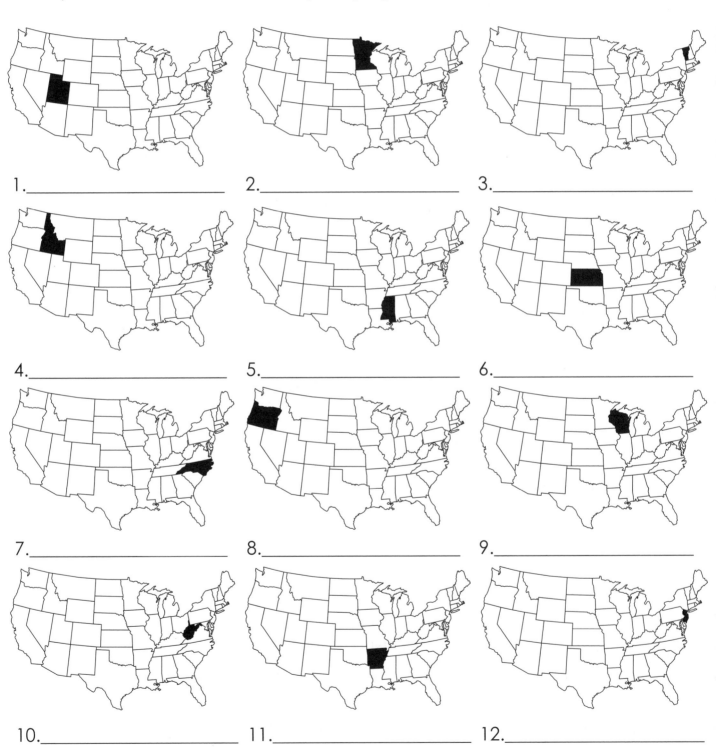

1._____

2._____

3._____

4._____

5._____

6._____

7._____

8._____

9._____

10._____

11._____

12._____

Shape Up!

Identify the shaded US states. Then, write each state's name on the line below its map. Use an atlas or the US map on page 45.

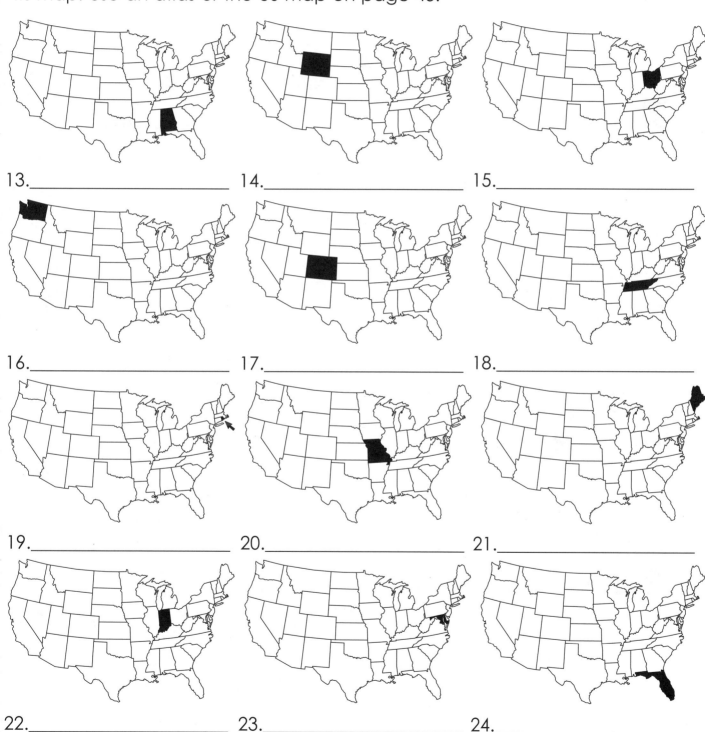

13._____

14._____

15._____

16._____

17._____

18._____

19._____

20._____

21._____

22._____

23._____

24._____

Shape Up!

Identify the shaded US states. Then, write each state's name on the line below its map. Use an atlas or the US map on page 45.

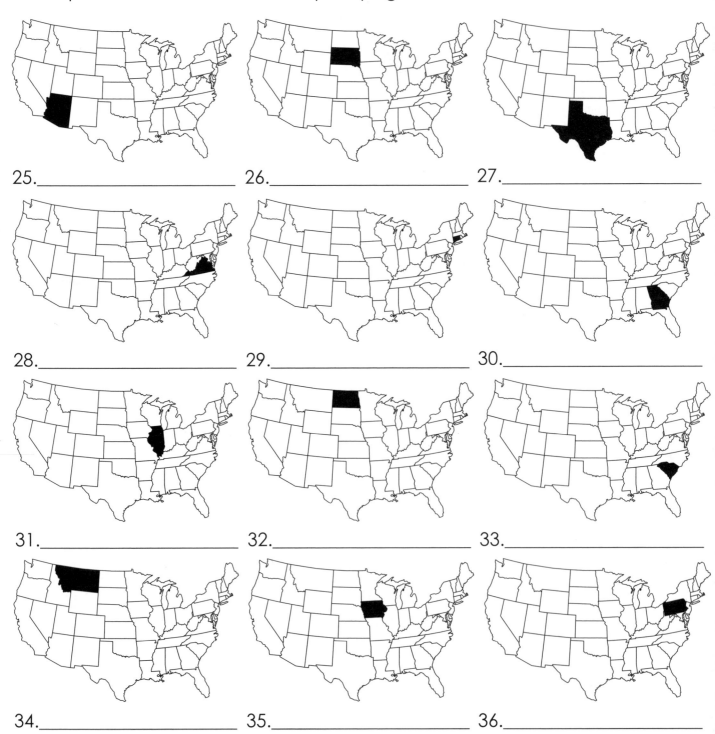

25._____ 26._____ 27._____

28._____ 29._____ 30._____

31._____ 32._____ 33._____

34._____ 35._____ 36._____

Shape Up!

Identify the shaded US states. Then, write each state's name on the line below its map. Use an atlas or the US map on page 45.

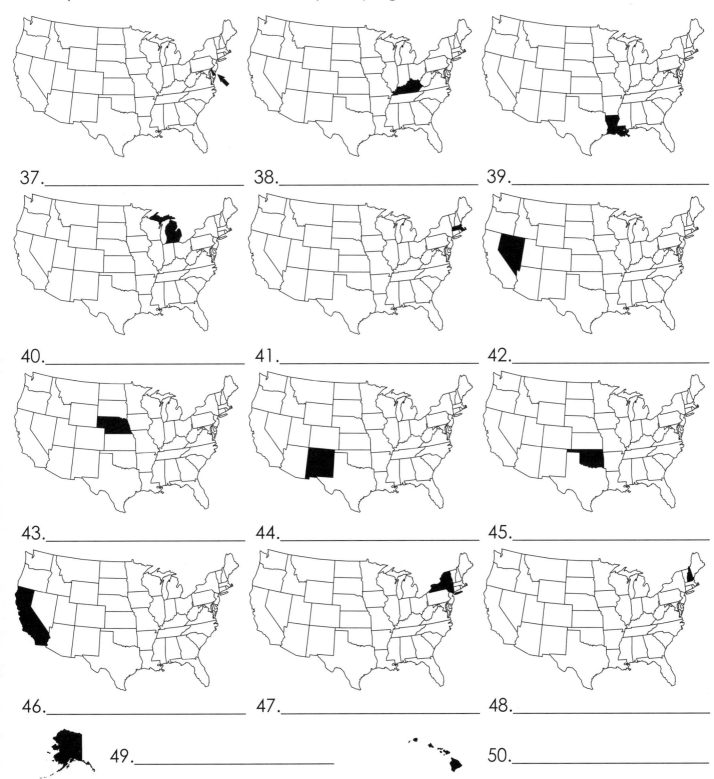

37._____   38._____   39._____

40._____   41._____   42._____

43._____   44._____   45._____

46._____   47._____   48._____

49._____   50._____

Fun with States

Answer the questions below about the United States. You may use an atlas for reference.

1. Which US states have exactly four letters in their names?
   _____, _____, and _____

2. Name two states west of the Mississippi that begin with O.
   _____ and _____

3. Which western state capital begins with an O?
   _____

   This is the capital of which state? _____

4. What is the capital of Tennessee? _____

5. How many states border Pennsylvania? _____
   Name them. _____ _____, _____, _____ _____,
   _____ _____, _____, and _____

6. Which west coast states border the Pacific Ocean?
   _____, _____, and _____

7. Which two states border Florida?_____ and _____

8. What is the capital of Nevada? _____ _____

9. This state, whose capital is Tallahassee, extends into the Atlantic Ocean.
   What is the name of this state? _____

Name_____

What Do You Know?

Read the statements below and decide if they are true or false. Write a "T" in the blank for a true statement and an "F" for a false statement. Change any false statements to make them true. You may use an atlas.

_____ 1. Florida is next to the Atlantic Ocean.

_____ 2. North Carolina is south of South Carolina.

_____ 3. New York is the name of both a city and a state.

_____ 4. Washington state is the capital of the United States.

_____ 5. Houston is the largest state in the continental United States.

_____ 6. Maine is north of Canada.

_____ 7. Minnesota is bordered by Canada to the north.

_____ 8. West Virginia and Virginia are both states.

_____ 9. Colorado is south of New Mexico.

_____ 10. Hawaii is a set of islands off of the coast of California.

_____ 11. Las Vegas is a state in the western United States.

_____ 12. Portland is a state north of California.

_____ 13. Alaska is west of Canada.

Name that Capital!

Below is a map of the United States with a star on each state capital. Write the name of each capital beside its number below. Use an atlas if necessary.

1. _____
2. _____
3. _____
4. _____
5. _____
6. _____
7. _____
8. _____
9. _____
10. _____
11. _____
12. _____
13. _____

14. _____
15. _____
16. _____
17. _____
18. _____
19. _____
20. _____
21. _____
22. _____
23. _____
24. _____
25. _____
26. _____

27. _____
28. _____
29. _____
30. _____
31. _____
32. _____
33. _____
34. _____
35. _____
36. _____
37. _____
38. _____
39. _____

40. _____
41. _____
42. _____
43. _____
44. _____
45. _____
46. _____
47. _____
48. _____
49. _____
50. _____

What's Your Zone?

The United States has four main time zones, as well as time zones for Alaska and Hawaii. Look at the time zone map below and answer the questions as if you live in New York.

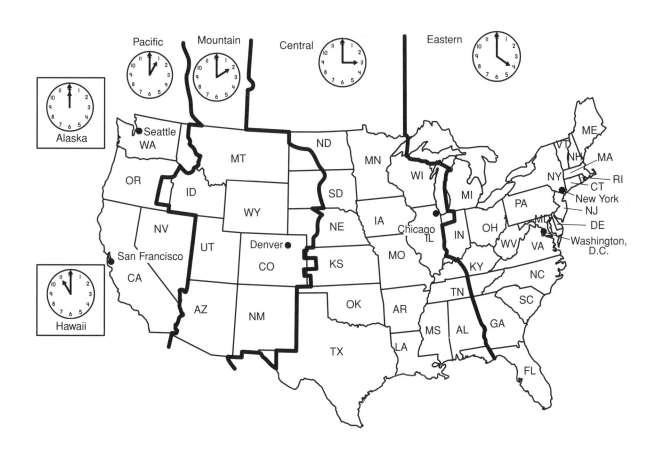

1. You live in the _____ time zone.
2. You call a friend in Denver at 8:00 A.M. eastern time. What time is it in Denver? _____
3. If your aunt in San Francisco calls you at 10:00 P.M. eastern time, what time is it in San Francisco? _____
4. A friend in Chicago needs to call your father in New York at 2:00 P.M. eastern time. What time should he call? _____
5. If you want to talk to someone in Washington, D.C., at 4:00 P.M., what time should you place your call? _____
6. Your friend in Hawaii wants to talk to you at 9:00 P.M. eastern time. What time should he call? _____

Name_____

Tell the Truth!

Using what you have learned about maps so far, answer the true/false questions below. Place a "T" in the blank for a true statement or an "F" for a false statement.

_____ 1. A political map shows land features such as mountains.

_____ 2. Lines of latitude run north and south.

_____ 3. The equator is 0° latitude.

_____ 4. An area of low pressure might be featured on a weather map.

_____ 5. A peninsula is surrounded by water on all sides.

_____ 6. A compass rose has only four directions.

_____ 7. A scale is used to show direction.

_____ 8. A physical map shows features such as mountains.

_____ 9. North, south, east, and west are cardinal directions.

_____ 10. The prime meridian is 0° longitude.

_____ 11. The United States has only three time zones.

_____ 12. Lines of longitude run north and south.

_____ 13. There are six continents on Earth.

_____ 14. There are four oceans on Earth.

_____ 15. The north pole is 90° north.

_____ 16. A plateau is a high landform that is flat on top.

_____ 17. A grid and coordinates are used to help find a particular location on a map.

_____ 18. The south pole is located in the northern hemisphere.

_____ 19. Road maps are used to predict the weather.

_____ 20. An ocean is the largest body of water on Earth.

Name That Map!

Each statement below describes a situation in which you need to get information from a map. Read each statement and circle the type of map that would be most helpful in each situation.

1. You need to know how many inches of rain fall in Hawaii annually.
   - A. political map
   - B. physical map
   - C. precipitation map
   - D. product map

2. Your teacher wants you to find out if sugar cane is grown in Louisiana.
   - A. physical map
   - B. product map
   - C. political map
   - D. weather map

3. Your family is taking a trip from New Mexico to Oregon. You want to know how many mountains you will cross.
   - A. physical map
   - B. political map
   - C. product map
   - D. precipitation map

4. You are reading an article about fishing in the United States. What type of map would best help you locate lakes and rivers for fishing?
   - A. product map
   - B. precipitation map
   - C. weather map
   - D. physical map

5. Your dad must go to Los Angeles for three days. He wants to know what the weather will be.
   - A. precipitation map
   - B. product map
   - C. weather map
   - D. physical map

6. You want to find out if Florida produces more cattle than Texas.
   - A. weather map
   - B. political map
   - C. product map
   - D. physical map

7. You want to know what the capital of Minnesota is.
   - A. political map
   - B. physical map
   - C. product map
   - D. precipitation map

Crossword Review

Test your map skills! Read the clues below to fill in the crossword puzzle.

Across

1. Half of a globe
4. A spherical representation of Earth
6. The direction at the top of a compass rose
8. This is used to show distance on a map.
11. The part of the map that tells what the symbols mean
12. The path to and from a location
16. A tool that shows directions on a map
17. A grid and coordinates help find this on a map.

Down

2. A map that shows governmental divisions of land such as states and countries
3. A large land mass on Earth; there are seven of them
5. A pattern of sections that are numbered and lettered on a map
7. A map of the inside of a building or house
9. A map that shows land features
10. This is what the compass rose shows on a map.
13. A picture in a map key that represents an object on a map
14. The largest type of body of water on Earth
15. A map that shows crops or goods produced in an area

 Map Skills—Grade 4

Map of the United States

MAINE
Augusta ★

Boston
MASSACHUSETTS

Providence
RHODE ISLAND

Hartford
CONNECTICUT

Concord
NEW HAMPSHIRE

Montpelier
VERMONT

Trenton
NEW JERSEY

Dover
DELAWARE

Annapolis
MARYLAND

WASHINGTON, D.C.

Albany
NEW YORK

PENNSYLVANIA
Harrisburg ★

WEST
VIRGINIA

Charleston

Richmond ★
VIRGINIA

Raleigh

NORTH CAROLINA

Columbia
SOUTH
CAROLINA

FLORIDA

Tallahassee ★

MICHIGAN

Lansing ★

OHIO
Columbus ★

Frankfort ★
KENTUCKY

Nashville ★
TENNESSEE

ALABAMA
Montgomery ★

Atlanta ★ GEORGIA

INDIANA
Indianapolis ★

ILLINOIS
Springfield ★

MISSISSIPPI

Jackson ★

WISCONSIN
Madison ★

St. Paul ★
MINNESOTA

IOWA
Des Moines ★

MISSOURI
Jefferson City ★

ARKANSAS
Little Rock ★

LOUISIANA

Baton Rouge ★

NORTH DAKOTA
Bismarck ★

Pierre ★
SOUTH DAKOTA

NEBRASKA

Lincoln ★

Topeka ★

KANSAS

OKLAHOMA
Oklahoma City ★

TEXAS

Austin ★

MONTANA

Helena ★

WYOMING

Cheyenne ★

Denver ★
COLORADO

Santa Fe ★
NEW MEXICO

WASHINGTON
Olympia ★

Salem ★

OREGON

Boise ★
IDAHO

Salt Lake City ★
UTAH

ARIZONA
Phoenix ★

Carson City ★
NEVADA

Sacramento ★

CALIFORNIA

HAWAII
Honolulu

(not shown at proportional size)

ALASKA

Juneau ★

(not shown at proportional size)

Answer Key

Super Spellers (pg. 5)

Frank	Alyssa	Jeff
Karen	Drew	Beatrice
Sam	Judy	Devin

Wild Goose Chase (pg. 6)
The correct route should be traced on the grid.

Sophie's New House (pg. 7)
1. 2
2. main
3. 3
4. east
5. 5
6. east
7. no
8. upper

Captain's Log (pg. 8)
1. A-1
2. Orion's Belt
3. C-1
4. B-4
5. B-5
6. Milky Way Galaxy
7. A-3
8. Star Tower

Camp Getaway (pg. 9)
1. camp director
2. playground
3. pool
4. A-4
5. lunchroom
6. A-2
7. B-1
8. basketball court
9. concession stand

How Far? (pg. 10)
1. no
2. St. Louis Arch
3. Space Needle
4. 1,200 miles

Traveling through the Black Hills (pg. 11)
1. 71
2. 16, 18
3. 471
4. 40
5. 90
6. 40
7. 16
8. 44

Farmington Field Trip (pg. 12)
1. Laura Bradley
2. Farmington
3. 116, Trivoli
4. west
5. Smithville
6. east
7. Canton
8. 474

Platte Parade (pg. 13)
The correct route should be traced on the map.
1. Platte River
2. 96
3. 11, 12
4. 1150
5. 14
6. 15

Map the Solar System (pg. 14)
Planets should be drawn in the following order:
1. Mercury
2. Venus
3. Earth
4. Mars
5. Jupiter
6. Saturn
7. Uranus
8. Neptune
9. Pluto
Each orbit should be traced in a different color.

Mapping Products (pg. 15)
1. shrimp, fish
2. Wisconsin
3. Texas
4. berries
5. cotton
6. Wisconsin
7. Wisconsin
8. Wisconsin
9. Texas
10. Texas

It's Raining! It's Pouring! (pg. 16)
1. Hawaii
2. 25 to 200 inches
3. less than 8 inches of rain
4. more than 200 inches of rain
5. Kamuela
6. Flagstaff
7. 8 to 16 inches
8. 25 to 200 inches

Airport Delays (pg. 17)
1. no
2. snow
3. St. Louis
4. Atlanta, Detroit, Las Vegas
5. sunny
6. Los Angeles, Seattle
7. yes
8. No, each city has weather conditions that could cause travel delays.

"Weather" It's Hot or Not (pg. 18)
1. cold
2. rain
3. Buffalo
4. fog
5. warm
6. Minnesota (MN), South Dakota (SD), North Dakota (ND)
7. Fort Myers
8. Canada
9. Oregon (OR), Montana (MT)

Geographic Features (pg. 20)

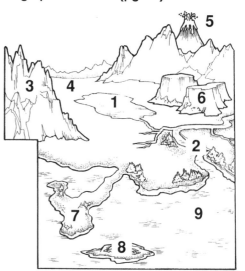

Answer Key

Matching Maps (pg. 21)
1. D, oceans
2. A, rivers
3. C, continents
4. D, states
5. B, mountains
6. A, lakes
7. B, cities
8. D, seas

Physical Features (pg. 22)
1. Lake Superior,
   Lake Huron,
   Lake Ontario,
   Lake Erie,
   Lake Michigan
2. Interior Plains
3. Rocky Mountains
4. Sierra Nevada Mountains
5. Atlantic Ocean,
   Pacific Ocean
6. Gulf of Mexico
7. Canada, Mexico
8. Mojave Desert
9. Hawaii

Mapping Africa (pg. 23)

Check to make sure that students have completed the map using the colors in the directions.

Mapping Montana (pg. 24)

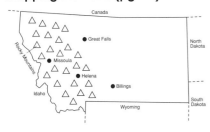

Check to make sure that students have completed the map using the colors in the directions.

Mapping Your State (pg. 25)
Maps will vary.

South America Scramble (pg. 26)

Scramble	Alphabetical Order
1. Chile	Argentina
2. Peru	Bolivia
3. Paraguay	Brazil
4. Brazil	Chile
5. Colombia	Colombia
6. Guyana	Ecuador
7. Ecuador	French Guiana
8. Uruguay	Guyana
9. Argentina	Paraguay
10. Suriname	Peru
11. French Guiana	Suriname
12. Venezuela	Uruguay
13. Bolivia	Venezuela

Where on Earth? Part 1 (pg. 27)
1. 90
2. equator
3. 90°
4. northern
5. southern

Where on Earth? Part 2 (pg. 28)
1. prime meridian
2. eastern
3. western

Two Hemispheres (pg. 29)
A. North America
B. South America
C. Antarctica
   western hemisphere
A. Europe
B. Asia
C. Africa
D. Australia
E. Antarctica
   eastern hemisphere

East and West (pg. 30)
1. western
2. eastern
3. eastern
4. western
5. eastern
6. eastern

Locating Landmarks (pg. 31)
1. Seattle
2. 41°N 74°W
3. Washington, D.C.
4. 38°N 91°W
5. 42°N 88°W
6. Philadelphia
7. San Francisco
8. 30°N 90°W
9. 41°N 113°W
10. Keystone

Locating Continents (pg. 32)
1. 40°N 100°W
2. 20°S 60°W
3. 0° 20°E
4. 60°N 40°E
5. 40°N 100°E
6. 20°S 140°E
7. 90°S 0°

Presidential Birth States (pg. 33)
1. Illinois
2. Missouri
3. Texas
4. Kentucky
5. Iowa
6. Massachusetts
7. Pennsylvania
8. Georgia
9. California
10. Virginia

Shape Up! (pg. 34-37)
1. Utah
2. Minnesota
3. Vermont
4. Idaho
5. Mississippi
6. Kansas
7. North Carolina
8. Oregon
9. Wisconsin
10. West Virginia
11. Arkansas
12. New Jersey
13. Alabama
14. Wyoming
15. Ohio
16. Washington
17. Colorado
18. Tennessee
19. Rhode Island
20. Missouri
21. Maine
22. Indiana
23. Maryland
24. Florida
25. Arizona
26. South Dakota
27. Texas
28. Virginia
29. Connecticut
30. Georgia

Answer Key

Shape Up! (pg. 34-37) continued

31. Illinois
32. North Dakota
33. South Carolina
34. Montana
35. Iowa
36. Pennsylvania
37. Delaware
38. Kentucky
39. Louisiana
40. Michigan
41. Massachusetts
42. Nevada
43. Nebraska
44. New Mexico
45. Oklahoma
46. California
47. New York
48. New Hampshire
49. Alaska
50. Hawaii

Fun with States (pg. 38)

1. Iowa, Utah, Ohio
2. Oregon, Oklahoma
3. Olympia, Washington
4. Nashville
5. 6, New York, Ohio, West Virginia, New Jersey, Maryland, Delaware
6. California, Oregon, Washington
7. Georgia, Alabama
8. Carson City
9. Florida

What Do You Know? (pg. 39)

1. T
2. F, North Carolina is north of South Carolina.
3. T
4. F, Washington, D.C. is the capital of the United States.
5. F, Texas is the largest state in the continental United States.
6. F, Maine is south of Canada.
7. T
8. T
9. F, Colorado is north of New Mexico.
10. T
11. F, Las Vegas is a city in the western United States.
12. F, Portland is a city north of California.
13. T

Name that Capital! (pg. 40)

1. Juneau, AK
2. Honolulu, HI
3. Olympia, WA
4. Salem, OR
5. Sacramento, CA
6. Carson City, NV
7. Boise, ID
8. Salt Lake City, UT
9. Phoenix, AZ
10. Helena, MT
11. Cheyenne, WY
12. Denver, CO
13. Santa Fe, NM
14. Bismarck, ND
15. Pierre, SD
16. Lincoln, NE
17. Topeka, KS
18. Oklahoma City, OK
19. Austin, TX
20. St. Paul, MN
21. Des Moines, IA
22. Jefferson City, MO
23. Little Rock, AR
24. Baton Rouge, LA
25. Madison, WI
26. Springfield, IL
27. Jackson, MS
28. Lansing, MI
29. Indianapolis, IN
30. Frankfort, KY

Name That Capital! (pg. 40) continued

31. Nashville, TN
32. Montgomery, AL
33. Columbus, OH
34. Charleston, WV
35. Richmond, VA
36. Raleigh, NC
37. Columbia, SC
38. Atlanta, GA
39. Tallahassee, FL
40. Albany, NY
41. Harrisburg
42. Annapolis, MD
43. Dover, DE
44. Trenton, NJ
45. Hartford, CT
46. Providence, RI
47. Boston, MA
48. Montpelier, VT
49. Concord, NH
50. Augusta, ME

What's Your Zone? (pg. 41)

1. eastern
2. 6:00 a.m.
3. 7:00 p.m.
4. 1:00 p.m.
5. 4:00 p.m.
6. 4:00 p.m.

Tell the Truth! (pg. 42)

1. F
2. F
3. T
4. T
5. F
6. F
7. F
8. T
9. T
10. T
11. F
12. T
13. F
14. T
15. T
16. T
17. T
18. F
19. F
20. T

Name That Map! (pg. 43)

1. C
2. B
3. A
4. D
5. C
6. C
7. A

Crossword Review (pg. 44)